I WASN'T CRYING OVER YOU

VINCENT K. HUNANYAN

For My Mother

CONTENTS

A FEW WORDS FROM YOURS TRULY

I must begin this volume and express my deepest gratitude to all the wonderful people who have shown interest in this work ever since *Black Book of Poems* saw light. I have had countless poetry enthusiasts reach out with the kindest of words that left me overwhelmed with humility and gratitude.

I never indented to add two short stories to *Black Book of Poems* but did so as a bonus for short story enthusiasts. I have chosen to include one of those stories in this collection.

The narratives you are about to read were drawn from my own experience and are told *almost* exactly in the way they happened. Out of respect to the people I once knew, some names and places have been altered. Some stories are products of my imagination and nothing else.

Having begun a tradition of adding something extra to my books, I have chosen to include two short one-act plays for theatre enthusiasts. Feel free to use the plays in any way you see fitting.

Again, thank you, and I sincerely hope you enjoy my work.

I WASN'T CRYING OVER YOU

I was seven, which meant that my father had been gone for seven years. Everything is easy at seven, the summers long and brave, and everything, infinite and unperturbed. My eyes were still too young to be malevolent and my tongue too pure to cause pain.

"Come on, I really have to go." I kept jumping up and down.

"I think I've lost the key."

"Very funny."

He *had* lost the key. "He" is my older

brother Charlie, and Charlie had just made us homeless. Mom was gone to bury our grandfather in the old country, and there was no spare key.

Charlie jerked the steel door as hard as he could, hoping for it to feel our despair and let us into safety, but the door proved relentless, and though I felt a stabbing pain in my stomach, I did not cry.

I was afraid of the dark, however, and though my brother pretended like he was not, I knew we shared the same anxiety. Outside, it was getting dark and my heart raced, and I looked at Charlie and asked what we should do.

After a few minutes of deep thought, Charlie concluded the best course of action was to retrace our steps. We went back to the playground where my brother had bounced around like a bunny on batteries, but it was dark, too dark to see, and there were a million scenarios in which the key was lost.

"The cops!" I yelled to my brother.

"Where?" Charlie turned around.

"Let's go to the cops! They will find mom!" I yelled again.

"Stop yelling."

"Let's go," I whispered.

My brother took me by the hand and led me back to the apartment complex.

"We'll sleep here." He pointed to the narrow space underneath the mailboxes by the entrance.

"We can't sleep here," I protested. "What if someone sees us?"

Charlie crouched below the mailboxes and pushed his body as far into the corner as he could, trying to glide into the wall.

"You can't see me, can you?" Charlie whispered, hiding his head in his palms.

"Yes, I can," I said.

"No, you can't; stop lying."

"Wait, why don't we go to the roof?" I said.

"Arch down here, before someone sees us," Charlie said, but I did not move.

"You'd rather sleep with homeless people?" Charlie went on.

"There are no homeless people on the roof! You need to know the code to get through the front door," I said.

"If you don't believe me, you can go and see for yourself," Charlie said.

"I will."

"Go ahead, but if you get stabbed by some maniac, I'm not going to save you."

The word "maniac" unsettled my already upset stomach.

"I'm going." I took my first step.

"As you wish." He wasn't buying my bluff, so I took another step and looked back.

"I'm going," I repeated.

"I know," Charlie said, still hunched below the mailboxes.

I took a couple more steps and reached the first floor.

"I told you," I shouted.

The only floors with working lights were the second and the fourth, making my heart drum faster for every anxious step I took, unsure of what it was I was trying to prove and to whom. I reached the

4

third floor. It was dark, and there were five more stories to go.

"I'm almost there!" I shouted in fear.

My brother had not said a word, and I began trembling, and then I heard the awful sound of metal bouncing heavily against metal. *The front door!* I flew down the stairs, scratching the side of my thigh on a rusty nail that had been resting there, waiting to tear my flesh ever since we had moved for the fourth time in two years.

Charlie was gone! My knees softened and I felt sick in my entire body. I ran into the street, shouting for Charlie, but nobody answered. I heard a noise from the playground and ran towards it, but he was not there. All I saw was a homeless man digging through the trash containers, talking to someone only he could see.

At last, I cried. I was homeless and "brotherless." I went back inside the building to weep in peace and had barely reached the first floor when a sudden, hysterical laughter came from behind me.

"Charlie! Charlie! Where are you?" My brother was imitating me, unable to stand straight.

"I'm telling Mom!" I yelled, as my sobbing

intensified and so did Charlie's laughter. In my distress, I was happy to reunite with my brother and finally calmed myself and dried my tears with the ragged sleeve of my dirty t-shirt and told Charlie that I hated him.

Having both calmed down, we decided to go to the police station; it was only a ten-minute walk, and though the darkness terrorized us, we found courage in being together.

ooo

"Where's your mother?" the cop began through his nose.

"Gone on business," Charlie said.

"Is there a phone you can contact her on?"

"No."

The cop inhaled deeply and rubbed his eyes for what seemed an unhealthy duration, stood up, took the Parliaments from the table and yelled, "Anton! Come here and take care of these kids," and left the station.

We sat in silence for almost an hour until Anton came in by chance, smelling the way my uncle did on weekends.

"What do you want?" the cop spotted us.

"We can't get home," Charlie said.

"Your folks kick you out?" Anton lit a cigarette.

"We lost the key," Charlie replied.

"*He* lost the key," I betrayed my brother.

The door to the station flew open and a tall, sturdy policeman with a thick beard and solemn eyes entered, dragging behind him a man who reeked of urine and could hardly stand on his feet.

"This is not a way to t-t-t-treat war heroes!" the drunkard mumbled. The solemn-eyed policeman pushed him into one of the three small cells where the prisoner repeatedly spat on the floor in protest and then proceeded to curse himself into oblivion, falling face down into his own saliva.

The tall policeman washed his hands in the sink by the cell and left the station without once looking at us. Anton looked at the prisoner in contempt, shook his head and cursed loudly and then turned his gaze back to us.

"Where are your parents?" he asked.

"Dad is dead; Mom is gone for the weekend," Charlie kept repeating.

"Any friends or relatives you could call?"

"No," Charlie said.

The cop looked at us with an expression that was a combination of pity and delight, and I thought of the time when Charlie and I stoned a mouse to death on our way to school.

"Maybe we could go to Mrs. G," my brother whispered to himself in an epiphany. The cop got up and stretched his back, moaning painfully.

"Go to Mrs. G," he said, stretching.

"What if she's not there?" I asked desperately.

"Then you're welcome to sleep with this son of a bitch." The cop smiled a disgusting smile, pointing at the sleeping veteran.

As we left the station, I turned to my brother.

"Why did you say that Dad was dead? He's not dead, he's just...gone."

"What's the difference?"

"There is a *big* difference."

"Shut up."

I did shut up. *Why was I defending him anyway?* He had betrayed me as recklessly as he had betrayed my brother, and I couldn't even remember what he smelled like.

The clock had passed twelve and it was much colder now, and we walked in silence, shivering through our thin t-shirts that we had worn forever. We reached the building where Mrs. G lived and knocked on the wooden door of her one-bedroom apartment that she rented out to a marine.

"Who is it?" Mrs. G asked through the door.

"It's us," we whispered in synch.

Mrs. G opened the door, put on her glasses that were hanging by a black chord down her heavy, wrinkled neck and squinted at us.

"What happened?"

"I lost the key, Mrs. G; we can't go home," my brother pleaded, ashamed.

"You little monkeys. Get in, get in." Mrs. G

gestured and I felt the warm, reassuring smell of her home and thought of Mom.

Mrs. G didn't ask any further questions but prepared a bed for us to sleep in, which for some reason was already warm.

"Mom is coming back tomorrow," I whispered to Charlie.

"I know. Go to sleep."

I turned my back to Charlie and closed my eyes.

"I wasn't crying over you," I whispered.

"I know," Charlie whispered back.

CLOSE COVER BEFORE STRIKING

She looked good in the coffin. Better than ever,
actually. The funeral folks had done a fine job
making her look more alive than she had ever been.
She had never had the slightest hint of femininity in
her. For his confirmation, she had come dressed in
a white t-shirt that said, ALL PRIESTS ARE
PEDOPHILES, and once her fourth beloved had left
her, she stopped wearing cosmetics altogether.

The funeral parlor was empty. Sitting in
complete serenity, Melvin wondered why he
couldn't cry. Deep down, he had to feel *something*.
He knew nobody had the right to judge him for not
crying, and though it felt natural to cry, he could

not.

All his life, he had tried to love her. He drew her landscapes and made her gifts out of anything he could find. He wrote her poetry, and he wrote her songs and played his guitar with much skill and effort and...she proved unlovable.

Melvin's father was not around; war had demonstrated the brute nature of men leaving him in a state of chemical imbalance, and he didn't spend much time with his son but preferred the company of his long-time friends, Mr. Daniels and Mr. Beam, until the two claimed his life on his son's seventh birthday.

Melvin's scars were *mostly* physical, and by her doing. She had once poured boiling water over him for his lack of vigilance after he had gotten robbed getting her pills. He had begun boxing to blame the bruises on the sport and reassure the troubled adults that everything was all right. When he was old enough to strike her back, he did not.

Melvin hurried to the bus station after the ceremony, with her remains in hand. He was running late, threatening to ruin his perfect record of twenty-two knockouts. In his ten years as a boxer, he had never been late to a fight.

His hand dug into the right pocket of his

threadbare coat and reappeared with a white matchbook he had been given at the parlor. "Think outside the box, plan your funeral- Kleinfeld & Sons Mortuary" was written in black. He flipped the matches, "CLOSE COVER BEFORE STRIKING. KEEP AWAY FROM CHILDREN."

The blue bus arrived at last, and Melvin got on. A sudden jerk of the wheels forced the urn from Melvin's grip; it fell to the floor and burst, and so did Melvin's heart as he fell to his knees, hopelessly trying to gather the remains of his mother, desperately thrusting the dust into the torn side pockets of his coat.

And then Melvin cried.

A stout toddler arched beside Melvin and stretched out the brown paper bag of his Happy Meal without uttering a word, but Melvin would not accept it. Instead, he stood up, emptied the side pockets where the remaining dust had stuck onto the cloth of his coat, and exited the bus.

He entered the ring where his opponent, a scrawny Irishman, was waiting in the corner. He began with a jab, moved his head to the left and followed with a violent uppercut. Another jab, feet swiftly to the left, right, then a hook to the ribs, and another to the head, and another one, and another one, and another one...

BREAKING AND ENTERING

Mom had been sick for two weeks. The reluctant breadwinner of the family was no longer capable of winning bread, and the food supply had become dangerously scarce. I was eight and my brother nine, and to our great delight, summer had finally made its comeback, and we were free from the angst of education.

Sitting by the swingers, bored and broke, our friend Boris, whom mom had marked into her book of bad influences, suggested we break into the neighbor's shed and steal the countless empty bottles of beer Boris had seen.

My brother and I rejected the idea, but the awful remembrance of going to bed on an aching stomach quickly turned the decision around.

"How we gonna get in?" Charlie asked Boris.

"There is a small opening in the back from all the rust, big enough for your brother to fit through." I scrutinized my physique to see whether I really was that small. To my great disappointment, I was.

"Are you sure he'll fit?" my brother asked.

"Why do you think we're taking him with us?"

Though my brother was only a year older than me, he was always closer friends with the neighboring hoodlums, and I was constantly made the third wheel.

"Do you want to do it today?" Charlie asked Boris.

"Tomorrow," Boris said.

We shook hands and headed home to check on Mom.

Mom's coughing was getting more hopeless and more painful, and it ached every inch of my tormented body. I took a few fearful footsteps and approached her. Mother's face was swollen and had taken on a yellowish color that hid the beautiful, subtle features of her countenance.

"Mom?" I whispered. She did not react. I softly squeezed her palm. "Mom?" She remained passive and I moved my head towards her face to hear her breath.

Charlie was in the kitchen, preparing porridge with tap water that tainted the taste of the oatmeal with a repulsive stink of chlorine and other toxins my nose could not identify.

"Is she still asleep?" my brother asked, turning off the stove. I nodded. "Here, eat." He stretched out our supper.

"I'm not hungry," I replied.

Charlie put the bowl of porridge on the table and opened the cupboard above the stove.

"What are you looking for?" I asked.

"I hid some sugar away in case of an emergency," Charlie answered, anxiously shoving aside cups and bags of spices that Grandma had brought from the old country but no one had used.

"It's gone," I whispered.

"What's gone?"

"The sugar."

"Why?"

"I was hungry," I said.

"What am I going to serve Mom?"

I shrugged my shoulders. "She won't eat, anyway." I paused. Charlie looked down on the ripped linoleum that we had found on top of a garage while playing Tarzan, and had brought it home and hammered it down, crooked and conspicuous.

"It's Mom's birthday tomorrow." Charlie looked up. I had forgotten.

"I know," I reassured him.

Charlie sat down and began eating the oatmeal, and I sat down across from him and observed.

"I'm not breaking into the shed," I said.

"Yes, you are."

"No, I'm not. You can't make me."

Charlie tightened his hand and raised his fist at me. "I'll beat you up!"

"I'll tell Mom!" I cried.

"If you tell Mom, I'll kill you and bury your tiny body under the shed!"

I flew towards the room where Mom was resting, yelling for her help.

I entered the room, catching my breath. She was still asleep. I cracked the door and stuck out an eye to try and locate my brother but could not find him. I opened the door and took a couple of timid steps into the hallway to see whether Charlie was lurking in the dark, waiting to jump me like a lion hunting antelope.

"I know you're there," I whispered, my blood gushing to my head. I took two rapid steps toward the light-switch and lit the corridor, but he was not there. I inspected the hallway carefully- his shoes and jacket were gone (which didn't necessarily mean he had gone outdoors as he had fooled me before by hiding his shoes and giving me a false sense of security to jump me when I least expected it). I tiptoed to the kitchen to make sure he was gone. He *was* gone. Having nothing to do, I put on my shoes and jacket and headed out myself.

When I reached the swingers, I saw Charlie and Boris sitting in silence. Something in my stomach told me to approach with caution, but I ignored the warning. As I drew closer, my brother nodded to Boris and the two flew on me like hyenas on a wounded animal making it impossible to escape, and I finally surrendered.

After a few punches, the two let go of my bruised body and sat down again. I lay in the sandbox doing my best to fight back the tears that were forcing themselves on me, but I didn't cry. Crying would have meant *they* had won. I stood up and wiped the sand off my jacket, picking dried leaves out of my pockets, pretending to be unhurt.

"I told you he'd come around," Charlie chuckled at Boris.

"I'm not doing it." I continued my rebellion despite the beating I had just received. Boris spit through the crack of his front teeth like a cobra and exhaled deeply.

"Why not?" he asked.

I wasn't sure why I had opposed the idea in the first place, but what had begun as an impetuous reluctance was now a matter of principle I could not comprehend.

"He doesn't know," my brother answered for me.

"I *do* know!" I tried to spit like a cobra myself, but the saliva hit the back of my teeth and drooled down my jacket.

"He's afraid," Boris intervened, "like a little girl."

"I'm not doing it because it's a sin!" I wiped the spit off my jacket.

"Do you even know what a sin is?" Charlie frowned.

"A sin is doing something wrong, knowingly." I recited my mother's words that had stuck with me ever since she had read us the child version of *The Divine Comedy*.

"Have you ever lied?" Boris asked me.

"Yes," I answered.

"Isn't lying a sin?"

"It *is* a sin!" Charlie shouted and pointed his index finger at me. "Sinner! Sinner! Sinner!" he kept shouting. Boris joined the inquisition. "Sinner! Sinner! Sinner!" They yelled in harmony.

"All right!" I shouted at the top of my lungs. So loud that someone yelled "shut the fuck up" from an open window.

ooo

The white nights had finally forced their way into the calendar, making the days go on for weeks and us staying out until it was safe to assume punishment, though this time around, the punisher was incapable of afflicting discipline, and we stayed out until our eyes grew red and our bodies begged for a break.

"Wake up." Charlie shook me. I opened my eyes and studied the thick fog that had embraced our apartment, unsure whether I was still asleep.

"What time is it?" I rubbed my eyes.

Charlie threw the shirt I had worn for days on my face and said it was time to go.

"Is Mom awake?" I yawned and smelled the shirt.

"Come on," my brother kept rushing.

"I need a new shirt."

My brother looked around the room and back at me.

"What's wrong with that one?" He pointed to the one he had thrown at me.

"Smell it." I threw the shirt back at him, aiming for his head but missing. Charlie picked up the shirt from the floor and put it to his nose.

"Wear it!" he ordered, throwing the shirt back.

"It smells," I argued.

Charlie walked towards the closet where Mom's clothes were neatly organized and our shirts shoved in like we didn't care; we didn't. Charlie studied the closet for a moment and took out one of my uncle's white tank tops.

"Here." He threw the tank top at me. "Now, shut up."

The top covered my body down to my knees, but knowing that arguing about its unfitting dimensions would only lead to violence, I refrained, and we left our home.

The fog had not settled and the mist lay thick, and I pretended like we were walking in the skies, defying gravity, like I did in my dreams.

"Charlie, we're walking in the sky," I whispered to my brother. He shook his head and told me to stop fooling around.

Up ahead, I saw the contour of what had to be Boris but also a slender figure standing next to him. As we drew near, my eyes reassured me that I had not guessed wrong, though the boy next to Boris was someone neither Charlie nor me knew.

"This is my cousin, Tiny," Boris said.

I wasn't sure whether this tall, skinny dope fiend was his kid cousin or whether "Tiny" was his nickname, but I didn't bother asking.

"You're nickname's Tiny?" Charlie raised his eyebrows.

"Yeah," Tiny's voice was deep and terrifying; he had to be at least thirteen.

"Why do they call you Tiny?" I jumped in.

"Because he has a tiny dick," Boris laughed.

Charlie smiled, but I didn't move a muscle for fear that Tiny would take it personally. The dope fiend looked aggressively at his cousin and ordered us to come along before the neighborhood got out of bed.

We walked through a narrow gravel path, and I saw needles and empty tubes of glue and avoided stepping on them. The shed was old and rusty; nails were sticking out in all directions out of its poorly maintained walls with spider webs and bird waste as the only decorations. We stood at the back of the shack, contemplating.

"Come here," Boris gestured towards me. "See if you'll fit through that crack." He pointed to the crack at the bottom right end of the shed where the wall ended and earth began.

"I don't think I'll fit," I said.

"Try," Boris ordered.

I hunched down on all fours and crawled to the crack, fearing the rugged edges of the rusty metal, but the opening was too small.

"See, I don't fit," I said.

Tiny lit a cigarette and approached. "Here," he put the cigarette in his mouth, squinting his eyes from the smoke that formed a duet with the fog and grabbed hold of the sharp, rusty end of the shed, "give me a hand." Charlie and Boris did as told and waited for further instructions.

"On the count of three," Tiny said. "One, two..."

"Wait!" I whispered as loudly as I could, almost not whispering at all.

"What?" The three looked at me dangerously.

"I think I heard something," I said.

"Just shut your mouth and get in there," Boris commanded. I looked at my brother for guidance and he nodded. The three raised the metal plate as high off the wall as they could, and I was in.

It was dark and dusty inside, and I tripped on a few bottles and tried to grab hold of something to steady myself, creating an offensively loud noise and causing the walls to vibrate. "Idiot!" I heard from the outside. I stood up, lifted my two arms in the air before me to try and shelter my face from any unpredictable objects and shuffled towards the small ray of light that was vaporing underneath the front entry.

I made it all the way to the front, uninjured, and pulled the tarnished lever and pushed open the door like the archangel at the pearly gates.

"Nice!" Boris' eyes lit up at the sight of the contraband, and I turned around to see whether our friend had exaggerated the value of the loot. I saw at least a hundred cases filled with empty bottles of beer and other beverages. There were boxes well worth over three hundred rubles!

"Hurry!" Tiny flicked his Parliaments. We got moving immediately and moved the loads of boxes in turns to the store across the street, running as fast as we could, risking everything.

"Did you break and enter somewhere, boys?" the short, blonde cashier asked. I panicked.

"Our parents drink a lot," Boris said calmly. She didn't care.

The heist was over in less than twenty minutes with all the bottles stolen. The adrenaline still pumped in my body as we met up by the swingers to count our earnings.

"All right, two hundred and eighty rubles," Boris counted aloud. "Two hundred for us," he pointed at his cousin and himself, drawing his finger back and forth, "and eighty for you."

"Eighty?" Charlie intervened.

"What's your problem?" Tiny took a step towards my brother who, to my great surprise and pride, didn't flinch.

"It's seventy each," my brother answered calmly, but I could see the twitch in his left eye, which meant the fuse was lit.

Boris looked at his cousin and smiled nervously. "Here's a hundred." He shoved two bills into the top pocket of my brother's jean vest and the two started towards the city. Charlie stood still for an instant, biting his lip until it bled.

"Hey!" he yelled after the two. "Hold on!"

The cousins stopped and turned around. Charlie charged towards Boris and slapped him across his mouth with an open palm. Boris jumped back in fright and looked to his cousin for guidance, but Tiny's imagination fell short.

"It's seventy each!" Charlie clenched his fist. Tiny stepped in at last.

"What's up?" He pushed my brother.

"It's one-on-one!" I stepped between the two. All fights in our neighborhood were to be fair; jumping someone with numbers was to have consequences.

Tiny remembered the code and stepped back and looked at Boris. "Get him." But Boris didn't move. Instead, he reached into the pocket of his shorts and took out two twenty bills and handed them to me.

"Here." He turned around to his cousin. "Let's go," and the two walked away, and Charlie nodded his head at me triumphantly.

ooo

"We'll have two hundred grams of these," Charlie pointed at Mom's favorite chocolates, "and two hundred grams of these." He pointed at *our* favorite candy behind the counter.

"Get some Hubba Bubba too!" I said.

"Mom doesn't like sweet gum," Charlie said.

"For us," I pleaded.

Charlie looked at me and at the cashier. "How much is it?"

"Your total is one hundred twenty rubles and fifty-five cents." The cashier fixed her hollow eyes on Charlie and chewed her gum loudly and indifferently.

"How much is the gum?" I asked.

"Fifteen." She kept chewing.

"What about the flowers?" he asked.

"You're right!" I had forgotten the damn flowers.

"Screw it, I know where to get the flowers," my brother told me bravely and turned to the cashier. "Give us that gum."

We stuffed our faces with the sweet, chunky bits of our favorite toffee, running out of breath as we unwrapped the chewing gum; life was worth living again.

"Where are we going to get the flowers?" I asked my brother with a mouth full of wonder.

"There." He pointed to a few tulips by our house I had failed to see. We hurried over and ripped out a dozen of them before anyone could spot us. They were soft, fragile and graceful, just like Mom.

We entered the room where she was still asleep and approached her bed and kissed her pinkish cheeks once on each side.

"Mom," my brother whispered.

"Mom," I repeated louder and shook her gently. She opened her eyes and smiled slowly and painfully. I stretched out the flowers and Charlie put the box of chocolates in her soft, paper-white hands, and she lay still and considered us in silence.

"Happy birthday, Mom," Charlie and I said.

She let go of our presents and grabbed hold of our hands as her eyes filled. She was awake at last.

LOVE IS DEAD

"Do you believe in love?"

"No, I don't believe in love."

It had stopped raining.

"Why?" She raised her head.

"Because love is dead."

"I thought *God* was dead."

"I don't know, maybe he is. I'm not Nietzsche."

They were lying naked in bed under the influence of cheap alcohol.

"What do you mean 'love is dead'?" She raised her head and looked at him.

"Wouldn't you rather lie in silence and enjoy the sound of the rain?"

"It's not raining anymore."

They were still for a moment.

"People are so desperate to feel something that they'll say and do anything," the boy said.

"Isn't that a basic human need?" the girl asked.

"To feel something?"

"Yes."

"Yes."

"So, what's wrong with that?"

"Nothing."

"I don't understand you sometimes," the girl said.

"Is there any water left?"

"Do you want some?"

He nodded, and she grabbed the half-full bottle on

the table and handed it to him. He raised his head and drank.

"Thank you." He exhaled deeply, gave her the bottle and fell down on the bed again. She put the empty bottle back on the table. He turned to her. "Love is kind of a cliché," the boy said.

"A cliché?"

"Yes. Love is supposed to be a powerful thing, right?"

"Right."

"And what's the definition of a cliché?" the boy asked.

"Something overused?" She answered timidly.

"Exactly. We can't replace words like love. Once they lose their meaning, that's it, they're gone, having become frivolous." He paused. "Forever."

"So, people shouldn't say that they love each other?"

He thought for a moment. "True love should not be dependent on words."

There was another moment of silence. It was

gentle, almost perfect. He was stroking her hair, and it was raining again. The blackouts caused by the unforgiving wind had left people in darkness and uncivilized. They didn't mind. They were lying next to each other, unfazed by the persistence of time and the dread of deadlines.

The raindrops were drumming forcefully against the dusty, thin window in broken rhythms. She was contemplating him in silence. His eyes were shut and a faint but untroubled smile was on his face. She softly put her lips to his head and gently kissed his temple, eyes, and lips.

"You're right. Love *is* dead," the girl said.

THE CHESTERFIELDS

Mr. Chesterfield was in good spirits on his way
home. After nineteen years at Winston & Winston,
he had finally been promoted. Everything in his life
was about to get bigger: his office, his paycheck, his
car, and perhaps even his flat.

Mr. Chesterfield was a man of forty years,
slightly obese and chinless. His turkey-like neck
stole much of the contour of his face and chin, and
if compared to an animal, he most closely
resembled a bird. Perhaps it was his sharp and
pointy nose that left one with such an impression.
His almost black, dark brown eyes were intelligent
and kind. He had a large birthmark on the left side
of his face, and narrow lips that became almost

invisible anytime he smiled, which he did unreasonably and often.

As he strolled the wet streets of London, Mr. Chesterfield contemplated the scenario in which he would break the news to Mrs. Chesterfield. To have a bit of fun, Mr. Chesterfield decided to play a little theater in which he was fired. He knew the news would devastate his wife, but he couldn't resist seeing the look on her face as he told her of his imaginary misfortune.

He had met Mrs. Chesterfield, who at the time was a thirty-nine-year-old widow, through his barber, who had claimed she was the perfect fit. After fifteen years together, Mr. Chesterfield was still unsure of what it was that made her perfect.

She was an ill-tempered and cynical woman who detested children and would always find something to complain about, despite the triviality of the matter. She constantly complained about their shortage of money but refused to get a job herself as she claimed to already have the job of the homemaker, though she barely cooked and had a maid clean every Monday.

A joke was spread that Mrs. Chesterfield's diseased husband had forged his own death to escape her, and what had seemed to Mr. Chesterfield like a bad anecdote, had become a nightmare.

Mr. Chesterfield arrived at his door and realized he had forgotten his keys at the office. He looked at his Timex Camper Watch: two hours, maybe longer, until she was back from her book club meeting she attended three times a week.

To save himself from the piercing wind, Mr. Chesterfield decided to wait at the Crazy Horse, a bar across the street he hadn't visited ever since he had gotten married. To Mr. Chesterfield's great disappointment, the Crazy Horse had changed its name to the Yelling Rooster and had become a gay club.

Mr. Chesterfield looked around before entering the club, took a few reluctant steps and approached the bar and sat down. No one looked *particularly* gay. The bartender, who was a young man in his late twenties and who had a pencil thin mustache and eyes that were a bit too close too each other, approached the guest.

"GT, please," Mr. Chesterfield ordered.

"Any specific gin?" the bartender asked.

"No," Mr. Chesterfield said.

The thin-mustached bartender mixed the gin and tonic and demanded to be paid. Mr. Chesterfield paid and sipped the drink. It tasted awful. He managed to drink four cocktails in a little over two hours. The drinks were taking effect rather rapidly, leaving Mr. Chesterfield feeling quite dizzy, but well.

"I was promoted today," Mr. Chesterfield bragged to the bartender.

"Good for you," the bartender replied, counting his tips.

Mr. Chesterfield frowned and hated the bartender, but nevertheless left a hefty tip as he exited the establishment.

The time had come to deliver the news. Mr. Chesterfield entered the apartment, took off his hat, coat and shoes, entered the kitchen and put the kettle on the stove.

"Dear, oh dear, where are you?" Mr. Chesterfield called with a feminine voice.

"I'm here, I'm here. What is it?" Mrs. Chesterfield entered the kitchen.

"Darling, please have a seat."

"What's going on, Tom?"

"I need to tell you something."

"What have you done, Tom?" Mrs. Chesterfield approached her husband. "Is that—is that gin on your breath?"

"Please, Emma, sit down."

"Since when do you drink gin?" Mrs. Chesterfield demanded.

"I need you to sit down, Emma. Please, please, will you sit down for me? Please?"

"Tom."

"Emma, please sit down."

"All right, all right." Mrs. Chesterfield sat down. "I'm seated. Now, what have you done?"

"I don't know how to tell you this, but," Mr. Chesterfield took a very effective dramatic pause and inhaled deeply, "I was let go today, Emma. I'm sorry."

Though Tom wasn't much of an actor, the words came out rather convincingly, perhaps due to the alcohol that aided him in this performance.

"Are you—are you taking the piss, Tom?"

"No. I'm sorry, Emma," Mr. Chesterfield said in a low tone and lowered his head, doing his best to suppress his laughter.

"Oh, you bloody idiot. You bloody, bloody idiot. What are we going to do now? What exactly are we going to do now, you bloody fool?"

"Emma, listen," Mr. Chesterfield was about to break character and come clean when Mrs. Chesterfield began.

"I think this is a better time than ever, then." She stood up. "I have been seeing someone." Mrs. Chesterfield took a deep breath of her own and exhaled heavily. "I have been seeing Richard for the past five years."

Richard was Tom's older brother who was much wealthier and more handsome and had a sense of humor that Tom was never blessed with. Ever since the Chesterfields got married, Mrs. Chesterfield had not stopped talking about Richard, demanding that her husband be more like his older brother.

The water had boiled and was now running down the sides of the silver kettle, in an intolerable whistle. In that instant, something inside Mr. Chesterfield urged him to grab hold of the kitchen knife and stab his wife fourteen times until she choked on her own blood.

Mr. Chesterfield picked the kettle from the heat, prepared his tea and sat down to drink it. The hot water burned his tongue and left it numb and useless.

THE BOY AND THE GIRL

The entire summer, they went on moonlight drives. The nights were usually too foggy to even see the moon, but he was too much of a Morrison fan to call it otherwise. They drove in the night, in her silver Nissan that was so old it was okay to smoke inside. The car was hers, but he would drive, and they would listen to "Hallelujah," both agreeing that Buckley's version was the most heartbreaking.

Most of the time, they drove around suburban neighborhoods, envisioning futures inside the fancy houses that nobody seemed to live in. The girl would explain with passion how she would decorate the house, the tiles of the kitchen floor, the pattern of the wallpapers, and even the design of the chandelier. There was always room for the boy in her future.

They sat in some diner, amidst the homeless and the insomniacs. Summer had long past.

"Had I the heavens' embroidered cloths, enwrought with golden and silver light, the blue and the dim and the dark cloths of night and light and the half light, I would spread the cloths under your feet, but I---"

"Please stop," the girl demanded.

He stopped.

"You're so full of shit."

He drank his coffee, unwilling to defend himself.

"You'll be all right, love."

The girl looked down into her cup and her eyes filled, and she sobbed and cursed the boy.

"I know," the boy said.

"Good." She wiped the tears that were running down her sleep-deprived, golden-brown face.

"I never wanted for any of this to happen," the boy said.

"I hate you."

"I know."

Outside, the rain fell relentlessly. The homeless were sleeping in their seats and the waitress walked up to the tables and woke them every five minutes.

"You want more pancakes?" He gestured for the waitress.

"Could you please stop talking?"

The waitress approached the boy and refilled his cup.

"Would you like anything else?" the server asked.

"Can we get some more pancakes?" the boy asked the waitress. "And the check, please."

"Of course. Anything for the lady?"

"It *is* for the lady," he clarified.

"I'm not a lady, remember?" the girl said.

"Stop that," the boy demanded.

The waitress disappeared.

"What are you doing?" he asked the girl.

"I don't want any damned pancakes."

"I already ordered."

She sat silent, scratching the silver spoon against the sugar in the bottom of the cup.

"You never spread your dreams under my feet, you know" the girl said.

"But I did, love."

"No, you didn't. You say you did, but you didn't, not really."

The waitress reemerged with the pancakes remarkably fast and put the plate in front of the girl and disappeared again.

"Eat the pancakes." He pushed the plate towards the girl.

"I don't want to." The girl stood up. "I'm going to the restroom. Please be here when I come back."

"Will you stop?"

The attendant refilled his cup and he paid the check. Outside, it had stopped raining but the homeless remained in the diner. *Go lightly from the ledge, babe. Go lightly on the ground,* came from the speakers. He approached the waitress and asked her to change the song but was told she had no control over it as all songs were playing in order but that she could lower the volume if he'd like. The girl came back from the restroom and sat down. The two were quiet for some time.

"Where do we go from here?" the girl said at last.

The boy drank what was left of his coffee, pushed the cup to the side and leaned back in his chair.

"I don't know," the boy said.

"And we can't fix it?" the girl asked.

"No," the boy said firmly. "I don't think we can."

The girl sat quiet and stared at the coffee cup on the table.

"Remember when you said that it was so strange of people to go from intense intimacy to never talk to each other again?" she said.

"Stop that."

"And then you said-"

"I know what I said," the boy interrupted.

"It was quite poetic," the girl said.

"It was then."

"Yes," the girl said, "and we're in the now."

"And we're in the now," the boy repeated.

"Would you do me a favor?" the girl asked.

"It depends."

"Could you please leave?" she said.

The two sat still and looked at one another for a long time until the boy stood up, put on his coat and left the girl among the homeless.

THE DEATH OF AUNT MARY

Aunt Mary had cancer and it was bad, and we had to see her before it was too late. We had to borrow money to make the trip to the old country because times were tough, and cancer didn't care.

We arrived at night and entered the apartment. I looked around and saw the old, bare, concrete walls and the wooden floor that had long lost its color and the innumerable buckets gathering water that dripped from the ceiling, and felt the sharp smell of fungus, and an overwhelming sadness came over me, and I sat down on the sofa that had been pushed to the middle of the room, away from the dripping water, and cried in silence.

The news had come without warning and too close to the end. She had experienced (as the doctor would later put it) intimate problems but was too timid to see a doctor for fear of gossip, and what had seemed like a minor offence had spread to her left kidney and turned into cancer.

Nobody told her of the tumor and that it was inoperable, but her brother insisted on keeping her spirits up, hoping for a miracle. He spent the last of her days injecting morphine into her delicate, thin arms against the pain that had become unbearable until her heart finally failed her, and no miracles ever occurred.

Out of his three sisters, she had been his favorite, and he loved her dearly and would always cry when drunk, bringing her memory to life, sobbing that she was a saint.

Growing up with a drunkard of a father, who was mostly absent, and a mother incapable of experiencing joy and affection, his sister was the closest thing to a mother he could hope for. She was very kind and calm, and she would never raise her voice or curse, and she *always* understood.

Aunt Mary had been married away unassertively and without protest to a man who loved her dearly and who was killed in Tbilisi only after a few years of marriage, leaving behind a widow with three small children.

When everyone refused to travel to the Georgian capital to claim his body, my uncle and father took it upon themselves to bring back the body. My father reassured my uncle during their return that it wasn't a corpse in the casket they were transporting but contraband.

When the end drew near, she had asked to be buried next to her father rather than her husband, but her wishes were not honored and she was buried next to the man she never loved.

We spent our last night talking until sunrise, and everyone cracked jokes to keep her spirits up, and she did her best to laugh to keep everyone's spirits up and asked my brother not to marry the neighboring girl, as she would become fat and dull like her mother. My brother promised that he wouldn't, and as we finished breakfast, I kissed and embraced her, saying that we'd see each other soon. She lay in bed and cried knowingly.

When she passed, I could not bear it and saw a priest, and he said that it was all part of God's plan, but I did not believe him.

THE RETURN

Charlie cried for days, blaming Mom for all the evils in the world, and we collectively and desperately implored her to find father. Mom made a few phone calls and received a phone number we prayed was his.

Charlie and I stood by the phone like statues when she finally dialed the number she'd been given. "Your children want to see you," she said. They spoke for a brief moment, and she hung up the telephone. "We will see him tonight," Mom said. My heart raced and a peculiar feeling of excitement and sickness came over me. I looked at Charlie and saw his eyes burn very bright and brown.

We were to meet at some market close to our home. It was winter and it was cold, and the snow lay rich and unrelenting, and I stomped with all my might to hear the snow screech and to irritate Charlie.

We approached the café and saw a man with a disproportionally big stomach that looked out of place on his otherwise thin body. He had a thick mustache, a red nose and sad, green eyes. He wore a leather jacket that looked too thin against the piercing wind, a pair of brown pants and black brogues. On his head, which was mostly bald, rested a checkered, newsboy hat.

We walked for a long time, and he said that we looked healthy and that mom had not lost her beauty, and she smiled and said that true beauty never faded. We went on walking in the wind, and when it was time to part, he said he would come and see us on the weekend.

On our way back, Charlie and I clung onto our mother like pandas, repeatedly asking whether he would come over for Saturday like he had promised and Mom said she thought he would.

Saturday came, but he didn't, and we cried inconsolably and without hope. Mom baked honey cakes and we forgot our dismay for a while and drank tea and ate the cakes that would have tasted so much better the day after, had we not devoured them all.

There was a knock on the door the next morning, and we flew towards the sound, but Mom yelled for us to stay away, as we weren't allowed to open the door unless it was she on the other side. Mother opened the door and revealed dad, standing in his thin, leather jacket, with bags of groceries in his frozen hands.

We didn't approach the door but sat in the kitchen in silent protest. He walked in and put the bags on the kitchen counter, and the snow from the bags melted down the plastic and onto the linoleum of the table creating small ponds. He looked at us and said something funny, and we laughed and hugged him, and I could finally place the unidentified smell that had tortured my mind for years.

"Who wants pork chops?" he asked. We yelled "me" in unison and mom prepared the meat, and dad sat down and read the paper with a toothpick between his teeth. I did not know whether Mom was happy he was back, but I knew that she always put her suffering last and did whatever was necessary so we'd be happy, though I believed the idea of us being a family again comforted her. And for a while, we were a family again, and he kept coming more frequently with groceries, helping us with our homework and even teaching us chess.

The lights went out in the entire apartment one evening and we lit candles, and he said that someone didn't want him there. Every day, he grew suspicious of the neighbors, and his face would tense up, and he would stare anxiously at the door anytime someone knocked. When the lights went out for the second time in one week, he was certain it was because of him.

His visits became less frequent until one day, he stopped coming altogether and it wasn't until we were leaving the country that I saw him for the last time and cried with the same bitter intensity, as on the Saturday he didn't show.

COOL VIBRATIONS

The vibration of your phone goes off at exactly three o'clock, *post meridiem,* commanding your attention. It's an email about some offer from some website you visited, God knows when. Three hours, thirty-seven likes and fifty-five shares later, your email is still unchecked.

The paper is due tomorrow at nine in the morning, and you have just finished the introduction, hoping you put that fucking thesis statement in the right paragraph. You look at your phone to check the time: it's almost dinner and there is a notification.

At nine o'clock *post meridiem,* you set your

phone in airplane mode and put it face down on the desk. You shut your laptop and grab a pen. A pen! It feels foreign and out of place between your fingers, but you must focus! *Focus, you moron, focus!*

It is almost midnight and you have seven pages to go. You rub your eyes, feeling a little sorry for yourself, whispering that you didn't ask to be born and smell yet another cup of coffee that makes you sick, but your force it down, doing your best not to break.

- What if someone is trying to get hold of me?

- It's midnight.

- So what? People might need me. What if Mom tries to get hold of me?

- In the middle of the night?

- You know how paranoid she can be.

- You're right, she can be pretty paranoid. All right, check for any missed calls.

You turn off the airplane mode and hear two-dozen beeps and feel an endless stream of vibrations, but there are no missed calls.

- There you go, no missed calls. Now put it away and write your paper.

- Wait! Mia has tagged me!

Mia is the girl you have a crush on and you believe she likes you as well; after all, she's tagging you every day.

You put the phone away; it is two o'clock in the night. You turn off your phone and say out loud for God and everyone else to hear that you *will not* touch the phone again until you have finished your paper. You pick up the pen and resume writing.

The word "appropriate" has been used three times in one sentence, and remembering the words of your English professor, you grab you *Oxford American Writer's Thesaurus* you have never opened before to find an appropriate synonym. The book is very thick and heavy and your mind is weary and your eyes, tired.

You open your laptop to hurry the process of finding the right word and notice a message from Mia: "I can't even…" with a link to some video on YouTube. You press the link but the "video is not available." As you move the mouse towards the corner of the screen to minimize the window, your eyes fix on a "suggested" video of that stand-up comedian you love, performing that sketch you've had in your head for days.

It is four in the morning and no coffee in the

world can keep you awake anymore, and you decide to sleep until seven, which will give you two hours to finish the paper upon your awakening.

You open your eyes and look at your phone: it's eight thirty and you have exactly half an hour until your paper is worthless and your GPA takes a dramatic dive. Your whole life flashes before your eyes and you envision yourself on the street, having squandered all hopes of a worthy life, rejected by friends and family, doing favors for drugs.

Covered in cold sweat, you jump out of bed to print out the paper before your life loses all meaning. After five dreadful minutes of weird noises and a bit of shaking, the printer prints out three pages of a diagnostic report and is finally ready to be used. You set the printing option to "black and white," but the machine refuses to print, as there is no *yellow* ink left. You eject the cartridge, blow on it, shake it, curse it for an entire minute and finally lick it, but it doesn't help.

You rush to the library ten minutes before the deadline. There is a devastating queue to the printer and you remember reading an experiment in which the subject was let to the front of the line after explaining *why* she needed to print before anyone else. Yelling with all the intensity that is left in you that your essay is due in seven minutes, you hear someone in front of you say, "So is ours, dude."

You try again, shouting that your entire future depends on this paper, but to no avail.

You enter the classroom at ten past nine with desperation oozing from your pores and notice the clock above the whiteboard; it's only eight fifty-nine. You puff out in relief and put the paper on your professor's desk but soon realize you have forgotten the "works cited" page.

Fearing a meltdown, you calm yourself, accepting defeat. At ten past nine, an old woman wearing leather boots and an overly tight dress enters the classroom and informs of a sick professor: the papers are due electronically before midnight.

You whisper a victorious yes under your nose, thanking all gods (the new and the old) and your guardian angel (who must be very tired by now) and look at your watch: almost fifteen hours until deadline. Let's go to the library and finish this damned thing!

New Tinder notification: "Send dp."

TERENTI

His name was Terenti Yachvilli, and he was an old, Georgian man who used to sit in solitude by the swingers holding his beautiful, handmade cane and smoke out of his wooden mouthpiece looking into nothingness.

He talked gently and in low tones, and anytime someone asked him for his name, he would carefully look up and slowly pronounce it in three parts: Te-ren-ti.

A remarkably thick pair of glasses rested on his pointy, red nose and enormous ears. He had a strong jaw, thick, white hair and kind, defeated eyes. He had been struck by a grenade in the Great

War, and it rang in his ears every second of the day, every day.

Terenti lived by himself in a one-bedroom apartment in the suburb of St. Petersburg ever since his orphaned grandchildren, Alexandre and Nikolai, were deployed, and it had been weeks since Terenti had heard from them. The newspapers told of an intensified conflict, and every day, letters were sent to mothers and fathers of Russia.

Terenti sat in his usual spot, on the very edge of the bench, and smoked his Belamorkanals, which were queer-looking cigarettes (called *papirosas*). They were mostly paper and very little tobacco, had no filters and smelled terrible. He always smoked the papirosa through a wooden cigarette holder as he looked into the vacuum ahead and murmured something under his nose.

It had been a very long and warm summer, and we played ball until it got dark and our stomachs could not take it anymore. Waiting for Charlie to finish breakfast, I sat down on the bench next to Terenti, who had insisted that I call him by his first name and never say sir.

"Hi Terenti, how are you?"

"As good as the Lord permits," Terenti said, slowly turning his sunburnt face to me.

"And how good is that?" I asked.

Terenti dug into the left pocket of his thick, black coat that looked too heavy for the heat, and reappeared with a broken papirosa.

"Why don't you carry your cigarettes in the pack, Terenti?" I asked.

The old man did not respond but lit the cigarette and blew out the smoke in an all too familiar way, and I inhaled the awful smell of the cheap tobacco and moved away from Terenti so Mom wouldn't smack me thinking I had smoked.

"And why do you smoke Belamors?" I asked. "My uncle says it's the worst tobacco money can buy."

"Habit," Terenti paused, "is the great deadener." He looked at me solemnly. "Do you understand?"

"Yes." I did not understand.

"It used to be the finest tobacco," Terenti continued.

"When?" I asked.

"Before the collapse."

"How old are you, Terenti?"

"I don't remember." He grinned slowly, and I saw his toothless mouth and remained uncomfortably still.

"Did you serve in the Great War?"

"Yes," Terenti said.

"Where?" I asked.

"Leningrad."

"Were you there under the blockade as well?"

Terenti took the remains of the cigarette out of his wooden mouthpiece, put the cigarette holder in his pocket and threw the bud in the sandbox and grabbed hold of his cane with both hands. Charlie approached the playground holding a ball with too many holes that would deflate on a regular basis, and a small, black pump to keep the ball alive every twenty minutes or so.

"Hi Terenti, how are you?" Charlie asked.

"As good as the Lord permits," I imitated the old man.

"Off to play ball?" Terenti asked.

"Yes. Do you want to come and watch?" Charlie said.

"Not today." Terenti smiled.

"Let's go. They're waiting for us," Charlie said to me, and we bid Terenti farewell and left him in his loneliness.

"He survived the blockade," I said as we approached the field.

"I know. He has a shit load of medals," Charlie said.

"How do you know?"

"Alex showed me," Charlie said.

We approached the field and shook hands with the boys, firm and friendly. I looked at Charlie as he was jumping up and down in the goal, unwillingly sacrificing himself to be the keeper, and I asked him whether he thought the brothers were coming back and he said that he did not want to think about it.

We played for hours, and when Mom came to the field to announce dinner, we said we weren't hungry, and when she asked what we had eaten besides breakfast, we lied and claimed our friends had brought sandwiches, as we continued chasing the ball through fatigue and hunger.

When it got too dark to see, we went back and

I saw Terenti on the bench and wondered whether he had been sitting there the entire day.

"Hi Terenti," I said as we drew closer.

"Did you win?" the old man asked.

"Of course," Charlie said.

"That's good," Terenti said and lit a Belamore.

"Can I have one of those?" Charlie asked and looked to our balcony to see whether Mom was observing.

"Sure." Terenti handed my brother a cigarette.

"You know she will smell your fingers, don't you?" I said to Charlie in our tongue.

"That's why you do this." Charlie looked around the dark playground and found two thin branches he picked up and held like chopsticks, holding the cigarette in between the wooden pieces, never touching it with his hands.

We had learned the lesson to keep our fingers free from cigarette smell after Mom had surprised us by not only smelling our shirts, but our fingers. She had smacked us across our mouths and we struggled to fight back the tears, not because the slap was painful but because it was she who had delivered it.

"Is it true they gave you a bunch of medals, Terenti?" I asked.

Up from our balcony, we heard our mother's cry and told her we would be home soon.

"Everyone got one," Terenti said.

"What did you do?" Charlie asked, looking at our balcony before forcing the smoke on his lungs.

"Prayed to God I wouldn't die," the old man said.

"Is it true your ears are ringing all the time?" I asked Terenti, and Charlie looked at me and shook his head in disapproval of my question.

"Yes, but nobody has been answering for fifty years!" Terenti said and I saw him laugh for the first time and chuckled myself, insincerely and out of courtesy.

"What about the Blockade?" Charlie said and looked up at our balcony once again before putting the cigarette to his mouth.

Terenti's face became stern and his eyes took on a severe gaze, and he was looking into space again. We were all silent for a minute.

"Eight hundred and seventy one days of hunger," Terenti said.

"They didn't give you food? I asked.

"We lived on hundred and twenty five grams of bread," the old man said.

"Jesus Christ," Charlie said.

"Christ wasn't there," Terenti said and paused. "At first, the dead were buried with dignity and later they were buried in piles."

"Why?" I asked.

"Because even the gravediggers starved," Terenti said and lit another cigarette. "A frozen crow fell dead in the street in front of a crowd and they flew on the bird and fought each other over it. People looked like skeletons long before they died. More and more corpses lay in the streets and under the snow. And kids were orphaned by the hundreds, because mothers would give their rations to their children and starve themselves." Terenti pulled out his handkerchief and wiped his face. "And then the snow melted and revealed the corpses by the thousands."

Charlie and I stood quiet.

"Then they sent us to hold the front where I was shot," the old man said.

"Where were you shot?" Charlie asked.

"I received one right here." Terenti let go of the cane and pulled down the collar of his coat, and I saw a scar the size of a penny right above his collar bone and pictured the old man as a young soldier bleeding from his neck.

"It went right through," he said.

"Did it hurt?" Charlie asked.

"I don't remember," Terenti smiled, grabbing hold of his cane again.

Charlie plucked a few leaves of sorrel and chewed the sour plant to get rid of the tobacco taste and asked me to smell him.

"You're done," I said.

"Really?"

"Yes, chew some more," I said. "But don't pluck it here; dogs usually piss here."

"Yeah, right," Charlie said.

"They do," I said. "Even I have pissed here."

Charlie called me an animal and walked towards our house to pluck the uncontaminated sorrel. I looked at Terenti and saw he had not paid any attention to us but sat with a lifeless gaze that had become his trademark.

"Have you heard from the boys, Terenti?" I asked.

The old man sat like a statue, not moving a muscle, though I knew he must have heard me.

"Terenti?" I said.

"Yes?" The old man came alive and looked at me.

"How are the boys?"

"I don't know," Terenti said in a very low tone.

Charlie came back stuffing his mouth with more leaves than he could chew, and we looked at the old man who was no longer looking ahead but had turned his head to the side, away from us. He didn't move. Charlie looked at me uncertainly, and I shrugged my shoulders because it was too dark to see whether Terenti was crying or not.

"They'll be back, Terenti," I said. "I know it."

Charlie approached me and squeezed the back of my arm and whispered for me to stop talking.

Mom called for the second time but in a very soft voice, and we knew this was our last warning. We wished Terenti a good night, and he said we were good boys without looking at us and wished us a good night in return.

Autumn came and leaves fell, and I walked the crowded streets of St. Petersburg, and listened to the sound of wheels moving heavily against the wet asphalt and admired the way everything changed color in the rain.

Terenti had stopped coming to the playground, and I thought of Alex and Nikko and feared the worst. The old man had finally received a letter, but not from his grandsons. The department of war regretfully announced the death of Alexandre and Nikolai Yachvilli.

Terenti traveled to the front to gather the remains of his grandchildren, but the corpses had been badly mutilated, and it was impossible to say who was who.

GOOD BOYS DON'T SNIFF GLUE

"Is he living or dead?" I asked Cornelius.

Charlie and I were sitting on the wooden bench under the shade of the massive oak tree, playing twenty-one questions with our friend, Cornelius, who stood in front of us because it was his turn to think of a person.

"Living," Cornelius said.

"Bruce Willis," Charlie said.

"It's not your turn," Cornelius said. "I get to

go again."

"Was it Bruce Willis?" I asked.

"Yes," Cornelius said. "But I'm going again because your brother ruined it."

We had met Cornelius on the very day we moved into the neighborhood when he had offered to help us with the furniture. He was a skinny, pale boy, two years Charlie's senior and three years older than myself. He had trouble pronouncing the letter 'r' and had a slight lisp that made some of his sentences very difficult to understand, especially when he got wound up and irritated.

He had an older brother, and they were both good-hearted and generous and very brave, and they would always do what was right, upholding a very righteous code of conduct, no matter the outcome. Despite their virtues, Mom suggested we stay away from the two as she had seen them smoke and suspected the use of alcohol and glue as well.

"I didn't ruin it," Charlie said. "It was my turn, and I guessed your lame person." My brother stood up. "It's my turn," he told Cornelius.

"We're playing clockwise," Cornelius said.

"We have never played clockwise," Charlie said and pushed Cornelius towards the bench.

"Your brother is a real moron." Cornelius looked at me and sat down.

"I know," I said.

Charlie stood in front of us like a drill commander, holding a stick with which he drew phallic symbols on the ground while thinking of a person for us to guess. Cornelius lit a cigarette, and I saw a large scar on his left hand.

"What's that from?" I asked, pointing to his scar.

"Nothing," Cornelius said. "Well?" he looked at Charlie. "Are you going to think until dark?"

"I got it," Charlie said. "Go."

"Living or dead?" I asked.

"It's my turn," Cornelius said.

"No, it's not," I objected.

"We're *still* playing clockwise," Cornelius said.

"Since when?" Charlie asked.

"Since forever," our friend lisped.

Someone cursed in the distance, and we turned around and saw Cornelius' father approach the big oak tree that was protecting us from the heat. He was wearing an old Reebok track suit of many odd colors and a pair of dirty, old sneakers with laces that had once been white but were now as dark as the shade under which we played.

He walked uncoordinated and out of balance and spoke very loudly to himself. He came closer and stuttered for a cigarette, and when Cornelius took out the Marlboros from his pocket, he snatched the entire pack out of his hand, dropping half of the cigarettes on the ground. Ignoring the cigarettes on the ground, he put the Marlboros in the side pocket of his Reebok overall and demanded a lighter.

"What are you playing?" he sniffed, grabbing the lighter from his son.

"Twenty-one questions, sir," Charlie said.

"I already know the answer!" he exclaimed.

I sat silently, trying to avoid eye contact.

"It's…" our friend's father put the cigarette in his mouth and began counting on his hands, looking at his fingers as if he had discovered them for the first time. "Five letters!" He sniffed loudly and spit very close to us and blinked in a very rapid succession, still unsure whether five was the right number of words. "No, wait!" he chuckled. "It's four!"

We kept silent. Cornelius was looking down at the symbols my brother had drawn, hoping for the spectacle to end soon.

"It's C-U-N-T-!" the drunkard shouted and limped away, laughing at his own ingenuity. Cornelius kept looking down at the dirt, and I gazed at Charlie and he sat down next to us. We all sat in silence.

When we told our mother the story, she shook her head and finally forbid us from seeing Cornelius.

"But he's a good boy," Charlie pleaded.

"Good boys don't sniff glue when they are twelve," Mom said.

We tried to argue his innocence, but Mom remained relentless, and we avoided Cornelius for weeks. When he came to the playground or to the football field, we became cold and passive, and he would leave unaware, and we felt disgusted and hated ourselves for being such terrible friends.

ooo

It was a Sunday and Mom baked blintz that we drowned in condensed milk and washed down with strong, back tea, praising Mom's cooking abilities.

"There's more coming," she said.

"No more, please." I unbuttoned my shorts.

"What about you, Charles?" Mom asked and put two freshly-made pancakes on the tray in front of us.

"If I have another one, I'll explode," Charlie said and reached for another one.

There was a knock on the door, and Mom asked if we were expecting anyone. We shook our heads and she said we could go and see who it was, but only after we asked and peeked through the peephole. I approached the entrance and leaned against the door.

"Who is it?" I whispered.

"It's me," someone stuttered. I looked through the peephole and saw Cornelius and opened the door. He was holding his shoulders, crying and trembling terribly.

"What happened to you?" Charlie asked as he came to the door, and I feared that the boys from 54th Street had beaten up our friend again.

"My f-f-f-f-f-father," Cornelius faltered. "P-p-p-p-poured b-b-b-boiling water over me." His crying intensified and I grabbed his arm and pulled him inside the apartment and shut the door.

We walked into the kitchen, and I explained in our language to Mom what had happened. She smiled the comforting, compassionate smile of a mother and embraced Cornelius and kissed his greasy, black hair, and I felt my throat thicken, and despised myself more passionately than ever for having ignored my friend.

Mom asked Cornelius where he had been burned, and he pulled the right sleeve of his t-shirt and raised his pinkish shoulder to the light saying he had dodged his father just in time and only his upper arm was burned. Mom filled a plastic bag with ice and told him to keep it on his shoulder.

"Sit down; we're having pancakes," Mom told our friend.

Cornelius stopped crying and was much calmer now. He sat down but declined the pancakes out of politeness, but Mom insisted and served half a dozen blintz and prepared fresh tea. She served the tea and told Cornelius to be careful not to spill it and Charlie and I sat down next to our friend and told anecdotes so he could forget his dread, if only for a while, until it was time to return home again.

VINCENT K. HUNANYAN

SQUARE ONE: A PLAY IN ONE ACT

CHARACTERS

BOY

GIRL

[*PARK*- *A naked park with a classic garden bench in the middle of the scene.* **BOY** *is seated on the bench.* **GIRL** *enters and sits down next to* **BOY***. There is a long silence.*]

GIRL. Please, let's never do that again.

BOY (*stands up and crosses the stage*). It's not like I wanted to.

GIRL. I know, and I've been thinking.

BOY. What about?

GIRL. About what you said last night.

BOY (*firmly*). Good.

GIRL. I understand you.

BOY (*less firm*). Good.

GIRL. But you have to understand me too.

BOY. I understand you. I just think what you're doing is very unfair.

(LONG BEAT)

GIRL. And please, never curse at me again. It was very mean. And if it had been anyone else, I would have just walked away and never spoken to that person again.

(BEAT)

GIRL. And when you say something like that to someone, it's sort of a goodbye.

BOY. You brought it out of me.

GIRL. Just promise me that we won't do that again.

BOY. I can't promise something like that.

GIRL. I never want to go through that again.

(LONG BEAT)

BOY. Did you cry on your way home?

GIRL (*hesitantly*). You were so cruel to me.

BOY. It wasn't my intention to make you cry.

GIRL. I know. And I know you have been waiting for an answer. (beat) Everything I have told you has been true—

BOY. But?

GIRL. But I cannot change the past.

BOY. I really wish you didn't just say that.

GIRL. Why?

BOY. Because now, we're back at square one.

CURTAIN

REMEDIES: A PLAY IN ONE ACT

CHARACTERS

PATIENT

SHRINK

[A shrink's office. Two chairs on the opposite side of the stage. A small, glass table in the middle. On top of the table- Kleenex. Behind the chairs, up center, is a massive desk with an old-fashioned telephone. **PATIENT** *is having a session with his* **SHRINK.** *Silence. The ticking of a timepiece hanging somewhere in the office fills the stage.]*

PATIENT (*pointing at the ceiling*). Do you hear that?

SHRINK. Hear what?

PATIENT. The sound of dying.

SHRINK. Are you referring to the clock?

PATIENT. Have you ever read "If-"?

SHRINK. Let's go back to "the sound of dying."

PATIENT (*scratches the back of his neck obsessively*). Why do we always go back to things I don't want to talk about?

SHRINK. Is that something that has been bothering you lately?

PATIENT. Why the hell do you think I'm here?

SHRINK. Why *are* you here?

PATIENT. I was about to tell you, before you *(quotes with his fingers)* "went back."

SHRINK. Please continue.

PATIENT. As I was saying, have you ever read "If-"?"

SHRINK. The poem?

PATIENT. Yes, the poem. My brother emailed it to me *(pauses in seemingly deep thought and finally reveals his epiphany)*, probably to screw with me.

SHRINK. Why do you say that?

PATIENT. Say what?

SHRINK. That your brother sent you the poem to—

PATIENT. Screw with me?

SHRINK. Yes.

PATIENT *(hunches in his chair and focuses a pair of weary eyes upon the ceiling and then back at the shrink)*. I don't know, doc *(taking another deep pause)*, anyway, the point is that I've been haunted by this thing.

SHRINK. The poem?

PATIENT *(irritated)*. No, Freddy Krueger. Of course

the poem. Are you not listening to what I'm saying?

SHRINK. What is it about the poem that's bothering you?

PATIENT (*digging in his pockets*). The last two lines. (*takes out a piece of paper*) "If you can fill the unforgiving minute with sixty seconds worth of distant run (*clears his throat*), yours is the earth and everything that's in it, and which is more, you'll be a man, my son."

SHRINK. I see.

PATIENT (*irritated, squeezing the piece of paper in his hand and throwing it on the floor*). Oh yeah? What the fuck do you see?

SHRINK. You are clearly bothered by the poem.

PATIENT (*sarcastically*). Must have taken all the genius in you to figure that one out.

[The office telephone rings]

SHRINK. I'm sorry. I thought I had turned it off.

PATIENT (*a bit excited*). Answer it.

SHRINK (*a bit uncomfortable*). That won't be necessary.

[The telephone stops ringing]

PATIENT (*solemnly*). What if someone is trying to commit suicide?

SHRINK. There's a hotline for that.

PATIENT (*resentful*). There's a hotline for everything, isn't there, doc?

[*A long beat*]

SHRINK. Why do you feel you're wasting your time?

PATIENT (*stands up and crosses the stage, stopping downstage right*). It's raining.

SHRINK. Do you like the rain?

PATIENT (*absorbed by the precipitation*). It washes all the filth away.

SHRINK. I see.

PATIENT. You see a lot, don't you?

SHRINK. Please, have a seat.

PATIENT (*sitting down*). I have had these thoughts...

SHRINK. What kind of thoughts?

PATIENT. Bad.

SHRINK. Do you want to talk about them?

PATIENT. I can't go on like this.

SHRINK. Like what?

PATIENT (*wagging his finger back and forth, pointing at himself and the shrink*). This. Sitting here like a little girl, crying about my problems to someone who doesn't give a shit about how I really feel.

SHRINK. Is that how you feel?

PATIENT (*very irritated*). "Is that how you feel? Is that how you feel?" Is *that* all they teach you at Yale, or wherever the hell you got your diploma? Yes, I just told you how I feel! (*beat*) This isn't helping.

SHRINK. The therapy?

PATIENT. Yes. And the fact that I'm on anti-depressants is so depressing I can't even grasp it. How did it come to this?

SHRINK. We have come a long way since your first visit.

PATIENT (*smiling*). "If there's any illness for which people offer many remedies, you may be sure that particular illness is incurable."

SHRINK. Do you think that you are *ill*?

PATIENT. What do you care, anyway, as long as your bank account keeps getting filled?

SHRINK. That's not fair.

PATIENT. Exactly.

> [*PATIENT* stands up, picks up the wrinkled piece of paper he tossed on the floor and heads towards the exit]

PATIENT (*stopping center stage right, he turns around*). I'm leaving. (*As he exits the stage*) Fuck you very much, doc.

CURTAINS

ABOUT THE AUTHOR

Vincent Hunanyan was born in 1991 in Armenia and grew up in St. Petersburg, Russia. His parents divorced when he was a toddler, and he was raised by a single-mother.

In 2001, Vincent moved with his family to Sweden. After graduating high school, he moved to Los Angeles at the age of 19 where he attended Santa Monica City College and later UCLA, where he received a B.A. in English with a concentration in creative writing.

Hunanyan's first official title, *Black Book of Poems*, was published on the 21st of May and became an instant bestseller with raving reviews from critics and poetry fans.

I Wasn't Crying Over You is his first short story collection, mainly comprised of tales derived from the author's childhood growing up in St. Petersburg and his transition from childhood to adulthood.

Through an unforgiving writing style, Vincent brings back memories of war, alcoholism, brotherhood, love, loss and loneliness that he lays forth with minimum sentimentality and painful honesty.

Made in the USA
San Bernardino, CA
23 October 2017